# Ripley's SPIDERS
## and scary creepy crawlies

RIPLEY PUBLISHING

a Jim Pattison Company

**Written by** Camilla de la Bedoyere
**Consultant** Barbara Taylor

**PUBLISHING**

**Publisher** Anne Marshall

**Editorial Director** Rebecca Miles
**Project Editor** Charlotte Howell
**Picture Researchers** Michelle Foster,
Charlotte Howell
**Proofreader** Lisa Regan
**Indexer** Hilary Bird

**Art Director** Sam South
**Senior Designer** Michelle Foster
**Design** Rocket Design (East Anglia) Ltd
**Reprographics** Juice Creative Ltd

**www.ripleybooks.com**

ISBN 978-1-60991-115-7
10 9 8 7 6 5 4 3 2 1

Library of Congress Control Number: 2014939818

Printed in China
in June/2014
1st printing

# CONTENTS

PAGE 43

TWISTS

# MEGA MINI MONSTERS

## They're scary!

This jumping spider may look scary, but its body actually measures just 0.2 inches long. These harmless spiders are capable of jumping up to 40 times their own length!

**ACTUAL SIZE**

You have got the world at your feet—and if you look closely you will see it is crawling with some bizarre beasts of the mini variety. There are billions of bugs, slithering slimy things, sinister spiders, and creepy crawlies all around us, but how much do you know about them?

Join us on a trip into the dark dank soil, delve beneath plants, and peer into places you have never investigated before. We will show you the kingdom of the mini-monsters, where animals have giant crushing jaws, deadly venom, and powerful pincers. These creatures have a way of life that is incredible, awesome, and almost unbelievable!

TWISTS

These books are about "Believe It or Not!"—amazing facts, feats, and things that make you go "Wow!"

## Ripley's Believe It or Not!®

Dr. Mohamed Babu, from India, set up this ant experiment which shows their bodies changing color as they drink from different colored sugar water. Ants' abdomens are semi-transparent and absorb the colors they sip in the liquid.

Found a new word? Big Word Alert will explain it for you.

Look out for the "Twist It" column on some pages. Twist the book to find out more amazing facts about spiders and creepy crawlies.

# THEY'RE ANT-ASTIC!

## ...ngth in numbers

...there were a massive ...f-war between all the ants ...ll the humans in the world, ...e ants would win easily!

...are a whopping 1.5 million ...or every person on the planet. ...ether, they weigh more than all ...humans put together and can ...lmost anywhere on land, except ...icy Antarctic. Ants are sociable ...animals, and billions of them may share a single nest.

### Building a bridge
These weaver ants in Jakarta, Indonesia, clung together to form a bridge across a leafy gap that other ants in the group could walk across!

### Riders on the storm

Brazilian fire ants can survive floods by building themselves a raft—out of their own bodies. Half the ants become the raft, clutching onto each other, and the air between the ants can survive for weeks. The other ants climb aboard and the whole group can survive for weeks.

### UP CLOSE!

### TWIST IT!

Hungry Dracula ants feed on the blood of their young. They scratch holes in the larvae so they can drink the blood as it oozes out. The larvae survive the grisly attack.

If an ant gets dirty when it's been out scouting for food it waits at the entrance of the nest for its fellow nest-mates to lick it clean.

### AWESOME ANTS

A sting from a Maricopa harvester ant hurts as much as 12 honeybee stings. The sting of a bullet ant hurts as much as a gunshot, and fire ants deliver a burning bite that can leave scars. Ouch!

### ...afcutter ants

...Leafcutter ants can carry ...times their own weight! They ...travel far in search of their ...favorite leaves, which they cut ...down and carry back to the nest. ...he leaves make a fertilizer, which ...he ants use to grow a fungus ...that they eat—it's their only food.

A leafcutter nest contains more than five million ants.

Leafcutter ants lay down a chemical trail so they can always find their way back to the nest.

If a queen leafcutter ant dies, so do all the other ants in her colony.

### Ripley explains... Life in a colony

Ants live in big groups called colonies. Inside a colony, different ants have different jobs, and they even look different from one another.

**Queen**
This ant is huge, growing up to 2 inches long, and she's kept busy laying thousands or even millions of eggs a year!

**Female worker**
The other females in the colony do all the work, fetching food, looking after the queen, and tending the eggs and larvae.

**Males**
The males grow wings at mating time. Their only job is to mate with the queen, and then they die.

Colonies are rare in the world of invertebrates, but ants, bees, wasps, and termites can all live like this. Sharing out jobs can help a colony—and its members—to survive.

See the "Ripley explains" panels for extra info from our bug experts.

Turn over to find out why spiders and bugs are so scary...

# ARACHNOPHOBIA!

## Fearsome or fabulous? You decide...

Most spiders are smaller than a coin and totally harmless, but they strike fear into the hearts of millions. What is it about these eight-legged creepy crawlies that freaks people out?

A fear of spiders is called arachnophobia and it is one of the most common fears that people suffer from. Here at Ripley we believe it is wise to find out more about animals that frighten us, so let's investigate these creatures and discover whether spiders are terrible, terrific, or truly terrifying!

### Hairy legs
Spiders don't need noses or tongues because their hairy legs can smell and taste things!

### True or false?

| | TRUE | FALSE |
|---|---|---|
| Almost all spiders live on land. | ✓ | |
| All spider venom is dangerous to humans. | | ✓ |
| Some spiders have six legs. | | ✓ |
| Spiders are hunters that feed on other animals. | ✓ | |
| Spiders inject venom into their prey to stun or kill it before eating it. | ✓ | |

### SPIDER TALES

Spiders are older than dinosaurs and have been crawling around Earth for at least 300 million years.

Spiders can probably see in color, but like insects they probably can't see the color red.

Water spiders are able to live underwater. They carry a bubble of air with them, to breathe.

## TWIST IT!

## ...AND OTHER SCARY CREEPY CRAWLIES

### LOUDEST

Some of the loudest animals in the world are cicadas—beetles that sing by vibrating a drum-like plate at the base of the abdomen. A group of cicadas can be louder than a drill!

### FASTEST RUNNER

Tiger beetles can run at 6 mph, which is faster than lots of humans can manage!

### BEST SENSE OF SMELL

Male emperor moths can smell a female 7 miles away.

## Spinning machine
Spiders produce silk in the spinnerets at their bottom end, and use the silk to create extraordinary webs and traps.

## The eyes have it
Most spiders have eight eyes in two or three rows at the front of their head. Their big eyes help them to see at night and focus on prey.

## Huge brain
Small spiders have such a big brain that it spreads into their legs. They need a brain this size to be able to spin webs.

## Mighty mouth
Spiders have pedipalps, which look like little arms, and chelicerae (say chell-is-er-ay), which are pincer-like jaws, to help them get food to their mouth.

## WHAT'S THE VERDICT?

Do you give spiders the thumbs up? Do you agree with us that they are impressive animals with incredible powers and amazing lifestyles?

Do those long, spindly legs still give you the creeps, and are you still too scared to pick up a spider?

## HIGHEST JUMPER

Cat fleas are the world's bounciest invertebrates, and—for their size—jump higher than any other creature. A cat flea can leap about 200 times its own length.

## SMALLEST ANT

The tiniest ant in the world is less than 0.03 inches long.

## GREEDIEST

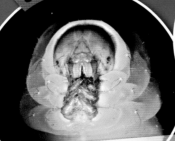

The caterpillar of a polyphemus moth eats 86,000 times its birth weight in the first two months of its life.

## FASTEST JUMPER

Click beetles can shoot up into the air at a greater speed for their weight than any other insect. This action is measured as "g-force."

# A WORLD OF CREEPY CRAWLIES
## Endless invertebrates!

Spiders and super scary creepy crawlies are not like other creatures. Most of them are tiny, but they make up the largest group of animals on the planet—invertebrates!

Scientists think that there may be more than 10 million types of animal in the world, and that at least 8 million are invertebrates—a group of creatures without backbones that includes all insects and spiders. Let us introduce you to the inspiring invertebrates!

## How many legs? →

Most mammals, such as horses, have four legs. Birds have just two legs, and fish have none. Invertebrates, however, can have anything from zero to hundreds of legs!

## Worms, slugs and snails

This group of invertebrates has no legs and soft skin. Earthworms live in the soil and breathe through their slimy skin. An earthworm has both male and female body parts.

Long slimy body

Slugs and snails belong to a group of animals called mollusks. Most mollusks live in the sea, but some of them enjoy life on the land.

## Insects

Insects have six legs and a hard outer skin called an exoskeleton. Insects are the most successful animals on the planet and, so far, one million species have been discovered. Beetles, bees, flies, butterflies, and ants are all insects.

Thorax

An insect's body is divided into three parts.

Head

Abdomen

A beetle has two pairs of wings. Its flying wings are tucked underneath a pair of hard, colored wings for protection. These hard wings are called elytra, or wing cases.

## Arachnids

Abdomen

This wolf spider is a large and fast hunter.

Head and thorax

Arachnids are a group of invertebrates that includes spiders, scorpions, mites, and ticks. All arachnids have eight legs, and an exoskeleton. We know about 30,000 to 40,000 species of spider, but there are probably lots more lurking in dark corners.

## Crustaceans

Crustaceans are invertebrates that mostly live in the sea, although a few species like to creep about on land. Some crustaceans have no legs, but others have 10, 14, or even more! Woodlice and beach hoppers are crustaceans.

The exoskeleton of a pill woodlouse (see left) is divided into many parts, or segments, so it can roll up and protect its softer underside.

## Centipedes and millipedes

These creepy crawlies have an exoskeleton and one species has as many as 750 legs! It's odd, but the ones with more legs often run more slowly than those with fewer legs.

An African giant millipede (see right) can grow to 12 inches long. It looks scary, but it only eats dead leaves.

A millipede's body is made up of lots of segments. They have two pairs of legs on each segment.

## Hard or squishy?

Invertebrates don't have a skeleton to keep their body strong, which is why they are small. Many of them do have an exoskeleton, though.

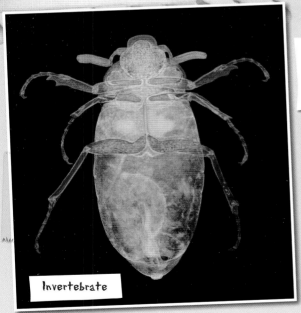

Invertebrate

This is an X-ray of a male cockchafer beetle, viewed from underneath. It has been colored to show the different body parts. There are no dark solid areas inside the beetle's body because there are no bones, just soft organs. The animal's legs are attached to the outside of its body, on its thorax.

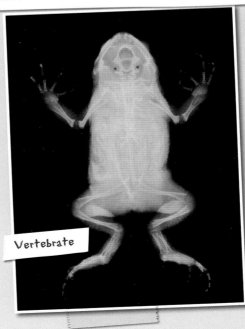

Vertebrate

This X-ray of a toad shows that it is a vertebrate—an animal with a backbone—as a bony skeleton is clearly visible inside its body. The long bone that runs from the head down the length of the body is called the vertebral column, or backbone. It protects the nerves that carry messages between the animal's brain and the rest of its body.

Long ago, people boiled and mashed snails to make paste to treat burns, and even smeared snail mucus onto sore skin.

Snails, slugs, and worms move by contracting and relaxing muscles in ripples, so their body moves forward.

Slime is so strong and stringy that a slug or snail can crawl along a sharp razor blade without being cut.

The world's longest worms can grow to 180 feet or more!

Tiny Japanese landsnails are tough little things. If they get swallowed by a bird they can survive the journey through the digestive system, and come out the other end, alive and perfectly well!

Believe it or not, a slug's bottom is just behind its head!

Scientists hope that one day they can use slug slime to make a glue that can be used to stick open wounds together instead of stitches.

## TWIST IT!

## HANG ON!

This is a no-win situation! A slimy ribbon worm might eat a cockroach, and a cockroach might fancy eating a worm (despite its foul flavor), but these two have got themselves into a desperately sticky state of affairs.

# SLIME, SLITHER, AND SLIDE

## If you can't crawl, creep!

If humans didn't have legs, how would we get around? We'd probably have to slide along the ground coated in a thick layer of gloopy slime. It's a gross idea, and that's one reason why legless mini-beasts seem so gruesome.

Slugs and snails are slime movers! As they creep, these soft-bodied mollusks leave a thick trail of sticky, slimy gunge behind them. The slime stops them from drying out, helps them glide easily over rough ground and stick to trees and walls, and helps to deter predators.

Worms can slither because they are covered in thousands of tiny hairs and a slimy goo called mucus. When earthworms get dry they coat themselves in mucus and have a little nap until it rains.

**GROSS!**

**Grub's up!**

Some young bugs don't have legs and have to wriggle and move. Called grubs or maggots, these supercreeps can't make a quick getaway, so they make a great meal for other animals. Witchetty grubs are baby moths, and they are big and juicy—so juicy that some people like to eat them!

**YUK!**

**BIG WORD ALERT**

**CONTRACT & RELAX**

The way muscles change shape so animals can move.

**Ripley's Believe It or Not!®**

A frog was peacefully snoozing when a slimy snail decided to take a short-cut—over its head! It took the snail eight minutes to slide over the frog, its only route across the branch.

# MAKING MILLIONS

## Taking over the world

Could bugs really ever take over the world? When one insect can produce thousands of offspring in just one year, are we at risk of drowning in a sea of spiders and scary creepy crawlies?

Spiders and insects usually live short, busy lives, and they don't often make caring parents. Their main aim is to eat and grow until they can produce young, and lots of them! They rarely spend much time looking after their eggs—they just hope that if they lay enough, some of them will survive.

## Super spidermoms

They may be in the minority, but some spiders make very good parents! Wolf spider mothers even carry their babies on their back for a week, while they grow bigger.

Baby spiders are called spiderlings. They look like their parents, but smaller. Their exoskeleton (outer skin) is soft, but it soon hardens.

## Big one!

Unusually, for insects, female tsetse flies produce just one egg at a time, and keep it inside their body while it hatches and grows into a larva. It feeds from its mother's body until it is big enough to be born.

I'm a BIG BABY!

**BIG WORD ALERT**

**LARVA**

A young insect.

# NASTY NUMBERS...

**40,000,000** The number of humans who accidentally eat roundworm eggs every year. Roundworms live inside pigs, but humans can get infected with them by eating undercooked pork.

**100,000** The number of eggs a tapeworm can produce every day. If an egg is eaten by an animal it will stay in the animal's guts and can grow into a worm measuring up to 100 feet long!

**10,000** The number of eggs some queen termites can lay in one day. The queen termite's job is to lay eggs for the colony every day for 15 years. When she gets old, the worker termites stop feeding her and she starves to death.

The mother can carry up to 100 spiderlings on her back at a time! They cling tightly to the little hairs on her body.

I'm a BIG MOMMA!

**1** Queen's stomach with thousands of eggs inside

**2** Queen's head

**3** Worker termites ready to catch eggs

A queen termite is 100 times bigger than the 1–2 million termite workers that look after her and the eggs.

**640** The number of baby aphids one aphid mom might produce in a summer. Female aphids are born pregnant. If all of their babies survive to have offspring there could be 1,560,000,000,000,000,000,000,000 new aphids in just one summer.

## Egg-sac-tly!

Mother spiders usually wrap their eggs in a silken bundle, called a cocoon or egg-sac. They protect the eggs from animals, such as birds, that might want to eat them, and when the spiderlings are ready to hatch, the mother can help them out of the cocoon.

About three weeks after they are laid, 50 or so little spiderlings will hatch from the eggs of this huntsman spider.

# EXTREME ARACHNIDS

## A ferocious family

Spiders belong to the arachnid family, and they have some creepy cousins.

All arachnids have six pairs of "limbs." The first pair of "limbs" are chelicerae, which are mostly used for feeding. The second pair—pedipalps—is used for touching and sensing. The other four pairs are legs. Many arachnids have venom (poison), and they are found all over the world.

## Harvestmen

Some arachnids are extremely revolting! An enormous group, or "cluster," of harvestmen with all those long, gangly legs is enough to make your skin crawl. They don't have venom but they do have foul stink glands that make a nasty smell to deter predators. It's thought they form massive clusters and use their combined stink to keep even big predators at bay.

A harvestman's legs are long and spindly and one pair is often used as a pair of "feelers."

A harvestman has just two eyes that are in the middle of its blobby body.

## Ticks

Ticks may be tiny, but these arachnids are terrible pests that live on animals and spread disease. They can't move by themselves, so they wait for a victim, cling onto it, and use their mouthparts to suck its blood.

This tick has been feeding on a dog, and its body is swollen with the dog's blood.

A sun spider has huge chelicerae (jaws) for killing prey.

## Sun spider

The sun spider's bite is deep, but not deadly. These arachnids have big jaws for crushing and killing, but they don't have venom. They use their pedipalps, which are equipped with suction pads, to grip onto their prey tightly.

The long tail ends in a stinger, which is used for defense.

## Imperial scorpion

The imperial—or emperor—scorpion is the world's largest scorpion, although it is not the deadliest. An adult has a bulky body and can grow to more than 8 inches long. Prehistoric scorpions, however, could grow to four times that size!

### ACTUAL SIZE

The body is shiny and black.

The pedipalps are large and strong and are used to kill prey.

# THEY'RE F-ANT-ASTIC!

## Strength in numbers

**If there were a massive tug-of-war between all the ants and all the humans in the world, the ants would win easily!**

There are a whopping 1.5 million ants for every person on the planet. Altogether, they weigh more than all the humans put together and can live almost anywhere on land, except the icy Antarctic. Ants are sociable animals, and billions of them may share a single nest.

## Building a bridge

These weaver ants in Jakarta, Indonesia, clung together to form a bridge across a leafy gap that other ants in the group could walk across!

## Leafcutter ants

Leafcutter ants can carry 20 times their own weight! They travel far in search of their favorite leaves, which they cut down and carry back to the nest. The leaves make a fertilizer, which the ants use to grow a fungus that they eat—it's their only food.

- A leafcutter nest contains more than five million ants.
- Leafcutter ants lay down a chemical trail so they can always find their way back to the nest.

# Riders on the storm

Brazilian fire ants can survive floods by building themselves a raft—out of their own bodies. Half the ants become the raft, clutching onto each other, and the air between them keeps the raft afloat. The other ants climb aboard and the whole group can survive for weeks.

**UP CLOSE!**

**TWIST IT!**

## AWESOME ANTS

A sting from a Maricopa harvester ant hurts as much as 12 honeybee stings. The sting of a bullet ant hurts as much as a gunshot, and fire ants deliver a burning bite that can leave scars. Ouch!

If an ant gets dirty when it's been out scouting for food it waits at the entrance of the nest for its fellow nest-mates to lick it clean.

Hungry Dracula ants feed on the blood of their young. They scratch holes in the larvae so they can drink the blood as it oozes out. The larvae survive the grisly attack.

## Ripley explains... Life in a colony

Ants live in big groups called colonies. Inside a colony, different ants have different jobs, and they even look different from one another.

### Queen

This ant is huge, growing up to 2 inches long, and she's kept busy laying thousands or even millions of eggs a year!

### Female worker

The other females in the colony do all the work, fetching food, looking after the queen, and tending the eggs and larvae.

### Males

The males grow wings at mating time. Their only job is to mate with the queen, and then they die.

If a queen leafcutter ant dies, so do all the other ants in her colony.

Colonies are rare in the world of invertebrates, but ants, bees, wasps, and termites can all live like this. Sharing out jobs can help a colony—and its members—to survive.

# WORLD WIDE WEBS

## Silky strong

**Spiders are nature's master builders. They not only build intricate and beautiful webs, they even manufacture their own building material!**

All spiders make silk. They can use it to make a highly structured web, a messy flytrap, or to wrap up their lunch to keep it fresh. The most impressive webs are built around a central point. Lines of silken thread come out of the center, like a bicycle's spokes, and spirals of silk are attached to them.

## Stretchy net webs

The net-casting spider weaves a sheet of stretchy silk into a mini-web, or "net." The spider hides, holding the net, and waits for a victim. It then rushes out, throws the net over its prey, wraps it in silk, bites it, and feeds on it.

A net-casting spider has a long, slender, stick-like body so it can hide out of sight while it waits with its net.

## Ripley explains... Web weaving

A web is made of three main types of silk thread—frame threads, radial threads, and spiral threads. The frame and radial threads are made of strong silk, but the spiral is made of sticky elastic silk so it doesn't break when insects struggle to escape.

Spiders have special glands inside their abdomen that make liquid silk. The liquid silk comes out of the gland and into a spinneret. From here, it is forced through a tiny hole, called a spigot. The liquid silk is pulled through acidic silk glands that harden it and turn it into solid thread.

### Step 1

The spider makes a long thread, which gets caught by the wind and sticks to a surface. It makes a second, looser thread attached to the first.

### Step 2
Next, it makes a Y shape to create the center of the web, and adds other threads to build the web's frame.

### Step 3
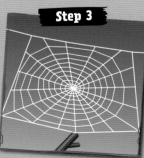
The spider weaves radial threads from the hub to the frame, and then adds sticky spiral threads around the radial threads.

A spider guides the silk out of its body using its legs.

## Big and tough

Giant orb-web spiders weave enormous webs that can span more than 6 feet across. Females can be as big as a human hand, but the males are much smaller. The webs are strong enough to trap small birds and bats.

This nursery web spider is keeping guard over her newly-hatched spiderlings.

The spider taps the silken threads to make her web vibrate, and tempt prey to come closer.

## Safety nets

Nursery web spiders hunt their prey rather than using a web to catch them. However, they do build large, messy, tent-like webs to protect their eggs.

## SECRETS OF SILK

Silk is stronger and stretchier than any threads that humans have been able to make. It can stretch six times its own length before it snaps.

⭐ Spiders can coat their silk with glue to make it extra sticky.

⭐ Silk gets ten times heavier as it turns from liquid to solid.

⭐ The best spider silk is stronger than human bone.

### Giant web

Spiders in Texas spun an enormous web that stretched for over 590 feet. Lots of different types of spider got in on the act and helped to make the massive bug trap.

# BRILLIANT BUILDERS

## And dastardly diggers

Spiders are wonderful with webs, but they are also good at creating other structures, as are lots of other creepy crawlies.

Birds build nests, foxes dig dens, and beavers build lodges out of sticks—but many creepy crawlies are also fantastic builders and diggers. Animals create homes to hide away from predators, protect their young, or store food.

This cautious spider is carefully opening the trap door to his hidden burrow.

## Trapdoor spiders

These clever spiders dig burrows to hide in, with silken lids and lots of silken "trip-wires" around the entrance. If a bug moves the trip-wire, the waiting spider leaps out and grabs lunch.

## Caddisflies

Caddisfly larvae live in ponds and rivers, and use silk to build themselves "invisibility cloaks" and nets. Their silken nets are used to trap food, and their "cloaks" are often strengthened with rock, sand, and bits of plant. This larva has used tiny snail shells to build itself a disguise.

## Paper wasps

A paper wasp chews up dead wood, and mixes it with spit to make a pulp for building its nest. The wasp constructs chambers, so an egg can be laid in each one. Each chamber is a hexagon, which is a great shape for building without wasting any space.

## Mighty mound

Termites build mounds using soil. Inside a mound, there is a complex system of tunnels for the termites to move through. There are other tunnels that allow fresh air to move around—like an air-conditioning system!

## Termites

Termites belong to the same family as bees and ants, and live in large colonies. They achieve some incredible building feats. One of the largest termite mounds found was 50 feet tall. That's like us building a house a mile high!

## Potter wasps

This potter wasp is carrying a ball of mud to add to its nest.

Potter wasps make nests out of mud, clay, and spit. They capture a caterpillar and sting it, so it stops moving but does not die. The caterpillar is then put into part of the mud nest—or "pot"—with an egg. When the egg hatches, it feeds on the caterpillar.

# DRESSING UP

## Masters of disguise

Many spiders and other creepy crawlies are kings of camouflage. One of these little creatures could be sitting right next to you—and you wouldn't even be aware of it.

Spiders and creepy crawlies are juicy treats for many animals, so some of them try their best to blend into the background to avoid being spotted and eaten. Some also use camouflage to catch unsuspecting bugs.

## Disgusting disguise

If you really want to stop someone from eating you, then making yourself look like poop is a brilliant move! If you ever notice a bird dropping crawling along the ground, look a bit closer. It may be a **BIRD DUNG SPIDER!**

**EWW!**

## Out of sight

Dressing up as a twig is a popular pastime in the animal world, which is no surprise given how many trees there are to hide in! Stick insects, birds, snakes, lizards, and caterpillars all have a go at this kind of disguise—but you need to be really eagle-eyed to spot a **STUMP ORB WEAVER SPIDER** such as this one.

Now you see me...

...now you don't!

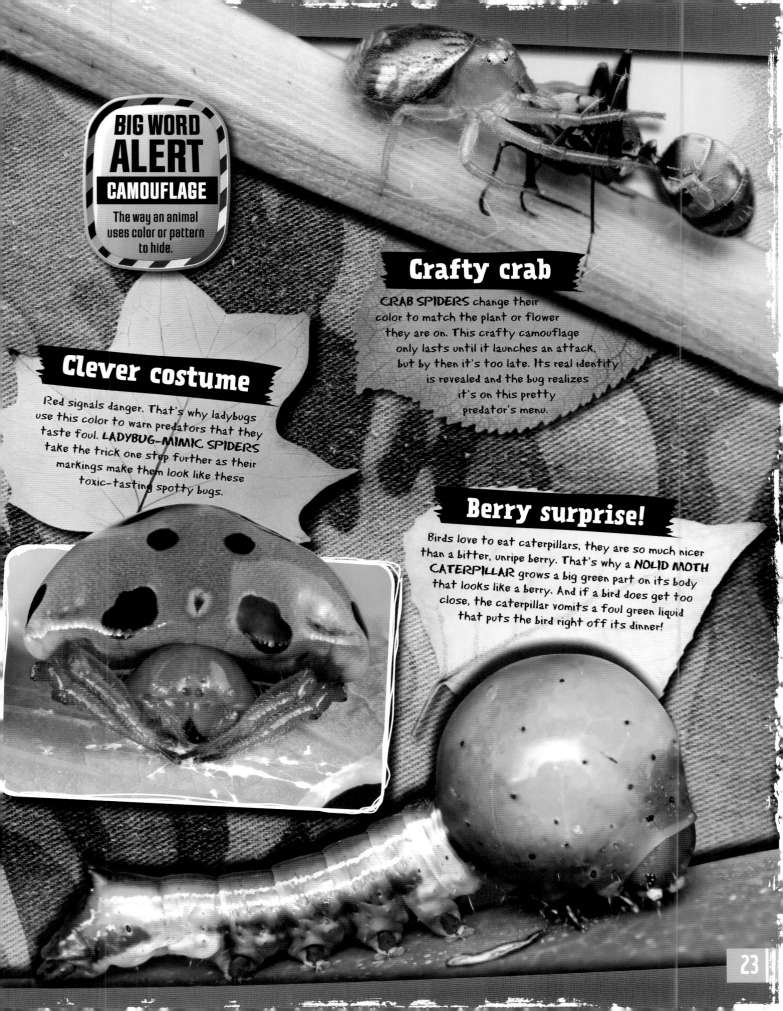

## Crafty crab

CRAB SPIDERS change their color to match the plant or flower they are on. This crafty camouflage only lasts until it launches an attack, but by then it's too late. Its real identity is revealed and the bug realizes it's on this pretty predator's menu.

## Clever costume

Red signals danger. That's why ladybugs use this color to warn predators that they taste foul. LADYBUG-MIMIC SPIDERS take the trick one step further as their markings make them look like these toxic-tasting spotty bugs.

## Berry surprise!

Birds love to eat caterpillars, they are so much nicer than a bitter, unripe berry. That's why a NOLID MOTH CATERPILLAR grows a big green part on its body that looks like a berry. And if a bird does get too close, the caterpillar vomits a foul green liquid that puts the bird right off its dinner!

# MY LIFE STORY — All change

Human children look like their parents—with two arms, two legs, and a head. In the weird world of insects, however, adults and their young can look so different you might never guess they belonged to the same family.

The way that a young insect changes into an adult is called metamorphosis—and, for some insects, it's a time when their entire body may turn into a gloopy soup and rearrange to create a new stage in the life cycle.

## The life cycle of a butterfly

A female lays her eggs on a leaf. An egg hatches and the butterfly larva (a tiny caterpillar) emerges, and eats and eats. A caterpillar can increase its body size 1,000 times in 2–4 weeks while it eats and grows. When it is done growing, it attaches itself to a branch.

**The caterpillar becomes a pupa. Its body is protected by a hard skin**

The caterpillar.

It becomes a pupa (a stage between larva and adult).

## The Life cycle of a Ladybug

Females lay little eggs on the underside of leaves. The eggs hatch and tiny black larvae emerge. As they eat, the larvae grow and molt their skin. When the larvae are big enough, they pupate (turn into a pupa). The ladybug's metamorphosis takes about one week. A pale adult emerges, and as it begins to dry it turns red and its spots appear.

### Pupation

Some insects go through a stage called pupation, and become a pupa, when they are changing from a larva to an adult. This stage can take weeks, or even years.

**Before**

An adult ladybug breaking out of its pupa.

**After**

### Circle of life

Adult
Pupa → Egg
Larva

### TWIST IT!

Periodical cicadas are large beetles that spend 17 years underground as a larva. They all emerge from the ground at the same time, creating swarms of millions of flying bugs.

Titan longhorn beetle larvae are gruesome grubs that measure up to seven inches long.

Giant water bugs carry their eggs on their back.

while all the body parts break down and reform into the adult shape.

The adult breaks out of the hard skin.

The butterfly adult dries its wings, and will soon be ready to fly.

An adult dragonfly gradually emerges from a nymph's shell.

## BIG WORD ALERT
### LIFE CYCLE

The story of how an animal starts its life, grows, produces young, and then dies.

## The life cycle of a dragonfly

The eggs are laid on water plants. The dragonfly larva that hatches out of the egg is called a nymph. Dragonfly nymphs live in water for about four years while they grow and develop. Then, they climb out of the water and crawl up a plant where they shed their skin and turn into adult dragonflies.

# BEETLE MANIA

## Tiny tanks of terror

Beetles are a very successful group of creepy crawlies—about one-third of all insects we know about today are beetles.

They have two pairs of wings, but the first pair has become hard and tough to protect the soft flying wings underneath.

Don't think I can't see you over there!

**BIG WORD ALERT**

**WEEVIL**

A type of small beetle with long mouthparts.

## Giraffe weevils

Giraffe weevils have weird long necks, just like their namesakes. A male's neck can be three times its body length, and he uses it to fight other males when it's time to mate. The neck of the female isn't as long as the male, but they are still able to use it to help roll a leaf into a nest, where they can lay their eggs.

## TWIST IT!

## BEETLE BANTER

Some beetles can glow in the dark! They make light so that their mates can find them in the dark.

Beetles never suffer from smelly feet. Their feet make a liquid that keeps them fresh and clean.

Bombardier beetles spray a foul toxic mix of chemicals at their attackers.

Cochineal beetles are crushed to make a natural red dye that is used in food, drinks, and make-up.

Bark beetles are no bigger than a grain of rice, but billions of them can destroy forests by munching through trees to lay their eggs. It is thought they have killed 30 billion trees in America alone.

## Jewel beetles

Jewel beetles are so beautiful they were once commonly used to make sparkly, colorful jewelry. Some of them only lay their eggs in burned wood, and they can detect the heat of forest fires 50 miles away. They are also attracted to the sound of the wood crackling and burning.

## Dung beetles

Dung beetles are fantastic at recycling. They collect animal dung (poop), roll it into balls, and lay their eggs in it. When larvae hatch from the eggs they find themselves safe and snug in a ball of delicious, smelly dung. It's a great place for a beetle to eat and grow.

# ACTUAL SIZE

## Not such a mini beast!

*It's hard to believe, but titan longhorn beetles can grow bigger than a small dog, such as a Chihuahua! The largest giant titan beetle found measured a colossal 7 inches long!*

### CRUSHING JAWS

Despite those massive jaws, titan longhorn beetles do not feed as adults. After a long period as larvae, the adults fly around just long enough to find a mate and reproduce, and then they die. They use their jaws to fight, and the jaws are strong enough to snap a pencil in half or break a human finger.

A whopping 7 inches long!

# TOP OF THE CLASS

## The biggest and the best!

There are big spiders, little spiders, colorful ones, and those that are so well camouflaged you may never ever see one. But which ones are the best in the field of arachnid antics and eight-legged attacks?

### Eye can see you!

This is a monster of a beast. It's a net-casting spider (see page 18), but is also known as an ogre-faced spider because of its fearsome face. It has such enormous eyes that when a torch is shone at them, they light up like the headlights of a car! These huge eyes help them to see better in the dark.

Spitting spiders win the prize for sticky surprises. Their venom glands have two parts—one part makes venom but the other part makes glue. When a spitting spider spots its prey, it fires two jets of superglue out of its fangs to fix the victim to the ground. Imprisoned by glue, the prey is finished off with a lethal jab of the fangs, and wrapped in silk to be eaten later.

### Take aim, fire!

### Longest legs

The prize for the spider with the longest legs goes to a type of huntsman spider with a leg span of up to 12 inches! Giant huntsman spiders live only in limestone caves in central Laos in Southeast Asia and they ambush their prey rather than build webs.

### Big appetite

This goliath bird-eating spider will try to eat almost anything smaller than itself—and as it grows as big as a dinner plate that means lots of creatures find themselves on the menu! Female bird-eating spiders can live for 20 years and have a leg span of 10 inches or more. Even their fangs are 0.7 inches long.

## SUPER SPIDERS

Widow spiders and funnel web spiders probably cause more serious bites to humans than any other spiders, but the most deadly of all are Brazilian wandering spiders. They are very aggressive and will bite rather than run away—and their venom can cause terrible pain and even death.

Bolas spiders don't waste their time building webs. They just hang a thread of sweet-smelling sticky silk beneath a branch and wait until a moth comes to investigate and gets stuck.

The fastest spiders in the world can cover 34 times their own body length per second when they run, but the golden wheel spider has a smarter way to get around. It somersaults its way across hot desert sand, covering 3 feet a second. If it gets too enthusiastic, it can die from exhaustion!

## TWIST IT!

# FLESH EATERS

**Spiders may be scary, and creepy crawlies may look like ugly little monsters, but without them our world would be piled high with dead animals—and plants would die.**

Spiders and bugs have some important jobs. Spiders eat the pests that would spread diseases to plants and animals. Worms, earwigs, and woodlice chew up plant material into compost so plants can grow. Bugs also eat dead animals and poop. Imagine a world without them!

## Rotten rotters

### Super slimers

Slugs and snails usually feed on living or decaying plants, but giant Spanish slugs also munch on the bodies of dead animals. When a group of them slithers onto a road to feed on animals that have been run over, their slime is slippery enough to make cars skid!

## FOUL FEAST

Maggots are fly larvae that feast on dead flesh and help dispose of animal bodies—it's nature's way of recycling. Unfortunately, lots of these maggots also like to eat our food. Let Ripley serve you up a delicious meal of unbelievable maggot grossness.

### On the menu...
Casu Marzu is a traditional Italian cheese that is served with the live maggots of cheese flies wriggling around in it.

### Really?
Yes. And what's more, the maggots eat the cheese, and their poo dissolves the cheese around them, making it soft and squishy.

### And for dessert...
The maggots can settle down to life inside a person's gut, causing a nasty disease called myiasis.

### Surprise!
The maggots can spring right out of the cheese and leap a distance of 5 inches toward your face as you eat!

## TWIST IT!

Creepy crawlies and other animals that feed on dead animals and plants turn them back into nutrients such as nitrogen. These nutrients are important for growing plants, and the animals that eat them (including us!).

Everyone knows that bees fertilize plants so that the plants can make seeds, but lots of flies and beetles do this important job too.

Up to one-third of the weight of a pillow can be made up of tiny arachnids called dust mites, their poop, and the bacteria that feeds on the poop. It sounds gross, but the dust mites do a great job of eating the dead skin that falls off your body while you sleep.

## KEY WORKERS

## Sexton beetles

Sexton beetles lead a very grave lifestyle. They dig a hole beneath a dead animal until it falls into their burrow. They roll it into a ball and bury it and a female then lays her eggs nearby. When the larvae hatch from the eggs, they feed on the dead body.

A sexton beetle can smell a dead animal a mile away.

## Seaside scrabble

Rotting seaweed doesn't just stink, it's also home to lots of bugs! Next time you are at the seaside, look out for kelp flies, tiny red mites, scarlet blood worms, beach pillbugs, and creepy little beach hoppers.

### BIG WORD ALERT
**DECAY**

When dead plants and animals rot and decompose.

## Don't leaf litter!

The ground beneath a tree is usually smothered in a layer of rotting leaves, fruit, and berries. Dig into leaf litter and you will find busy little beetles, bugs, and worms devouring the plant matter and turning it into soil.

# SUPERHERO SPIDERS

## Super spider skills

You know about Spider-Man and his amazing arachnid abilities, but did you know that fact is often stranger than fiction?

Real spiders have their own collection of superpowers. Follow these intrepid superheroes as they put their best feet forward—all eight of them—to do battle.

SPIDERLINGS (YOUNG SPIDERS) MAKE SILKEN PARACHUTES AND DRAGLINES AND USE THEM TO FLY THROUGH THE AIR. IDEALLY, THEY WANT TO DISPERSE AS QUICKLY AS POSSIBLE BEFORE THEY ATTRACT THE ATTENTION OF PREDATORS. THE WIND CARRIES THE SPIDERLINGS SOME DISTANCE, BUT A SOFT LANDING IS NOT ALWAYS GUARANTEED!

FLY THROUGH THE AIR ON A ZIP WIRE!

ZIP!

VERY FEW ANIMALS CAN WALK ON WATER, BUT RAFT SPIDERS ARE ABLE TO STAY ON THE SURFACE OF A POND. THEY CAN FEEL MOVEMENTS UNDERNEATH THEIR FEET, AND GRAB ANY FISH THAT GETS TOO CLOSE. THIS RAFT SPIDER IS SINKING ITS JAWS INTO A STICKLEBACK FISH.

AAAARGHH!

WALK ON WATER!

WOW!

**SUPER STRENGTH!**

**HEAVE!**

SPIDERS DON'T NORMALLY EAT SNAKES, BUT IF ONE LANDS UP ON YOUR TABLE, WHAT ARE YOU TO DO? THIS GOLDEN ORB WEB SPIDER CAN MAKE THE MOST OF HER GOOD FORTUNE BECAUSE SHE HAS SUPERHERO STRENGTH. SHE EVEN MAKES EXTRA-STRONG SILK TO HOLD ON TO THE SNAKE, SO IT CAN'T ESCAPE OR FALL.

JUMPING SPIDERS ARE SUPERB ATHLETES. THEY CAN JUDGE DISTANCES EXTREMELY WELL, AND USE THEIR JUMPING SKILLS TO POUNCE ON PREY. A SPIDER THAT IS JUST 0.3 INCHES LONG CAN JUMP MORE THAN 8 INCHES—THAT IS LIKE YOU JUMPING ABOUT 82 FEET IN A SINGLE LEAP—OR SPIDER-MAN LEAPING BETWEEN TWO SKYSCRAPERS.

**JUMP INCREDIBLE DISTANCES!**

WHEee...

**POUNCE!**

This Panamanian jumping spider is about to pounce on an unsuspecting cricket.

**GLADIATOR-STYLE!**

**GOTCHA!**

TARANTULAS ARE VERY HAIRY AND WHEN THEY ARE SCARED THEY SHOOT HAIRS AT THE FACE OF AN ATTACKER—THE EFFECT IS LIKE BEING HIT BY A CLOUD OF POISONED ARROWS. THE HAIRS ARE EXTREMELY IRRITATING AND IF THEY GET INTO AN ATTACKER'S EYES AND SKIN THEY CAUSE PAIN.

**TAKE THAT!**

**KAPOW!**

LONG AGO, ROMAN GLADIATORS TRAPPED THEIR ENEMIES IN NETS. SPIDERS DO THE SAME, BUT THEY USE INCREDIBLY STRONG SILK. IT'S LONG, BENDY, AND STICKY—PERFECT FOR WRAPPING UP THEIR PREY.

# SUPER SCARY SURVIVORS

## Staying alive

Invertebrates fight to survive every day of their lives. Many things threaten them, but avoiding deadly predators is number one on their list of top survival tips.

Spiders and creepy crawlies have different ways of staying alive. Spiders hide or use venom to kill their attackers, and creepy-crawly insects use a range of crafty tricks to keep predators away.

Armored cockroaches spray foul-smelling chemicals at attackers. The smell lingers for days.

## Alien attack!

Praying mantids avoid attack by scaring their attackers with a fearsome pose—they look like scary, long-armed aliens! They raise their spiky forelimbs, which are equipped with crushing claws, and show off their big bug eyes and bright belly.

Mantids make a crunchy morsel for bats, who are not so impressed by their alien impressions. Luckily, mantids can hear the high-pitched sounds made by bats. They don't waste their time posing, they just dive for cover instead!

## Strong suit

Creepy cockroaches are believed to be some of the most incredible survivors of the animal world. They can carry on living for months even if they have lost their head! They can eat all sorts of things, from other insects to paper, leather, and hair. They can even go without food for months.

# Gift giver!

Some female spiders take a fancy to males—but they don't just want to mate with the males, they quite like eating them too! Smart males give their female mate a gift of food so while she is busy eating they can make a quick escape.

**Food parcel**

This little male nursery web spider is hoping that his gift will make the female take pity on him, and get her lunch somewhere else today!

**Promise you won't eat me?**

## TWIST IT!

Sexton beetle mothers lay too many eggs for the food she can give them, so when she gets hungry she just starts eating her "extra" babies!

The bright yellow and black stripes on a hornet warn other animals to stay clear—this mini-beast has a massive stinger! Hornets use their scary stingers for attack and defense.

## SURVIVAL INSTINCT

Sow thistle aphids can sense an animal's hot breath. One whiff of it is enough to make an aphid leap off a plant and avoid being eaten!

## Squirting soldiers

Some termites can literally blow themselves up to protect the rest of their colony! Soldier termites stand guard outside the nest and if they are attacked they make a foul yellow liquid that they can spray at the attacker. It hardens into sticky glue when it makes contact, so the attacker can't move—but making the deadly liquid can cause the termite to explode!

**Workers**

**Soldiers**

Long nose termite soldiers are guarding workers in this nest. If any ants stroll by, the soldiers will spray glue at them.

# VICIOUS WITH VENOM

## Spine-chilling spiders

**Almost every spider in the world is a deadly predator that feeds on the bodies of other animals.**

Spiders are expert hunters, with speed, stealth, and a powerful bite that delivers a lethal dose of venom. Just one spider in your living room will devour about 20 flies in a few months—but the good news is that most spiders are completely harmless to humans.

### MONSTER JAWS

Bronzed tube web spiders have big jaws that appear to glow green in the dark!

Female spiders are more poisonous than males, except for the Sydney funnel-web spider.

Size isn't everything: furry bird-eating spiders—tarantulas—look like scary monsters, but they are quite peaceful spiders. Their bites may be painful, but they are not deadly to humans.

Scientists have found just one type of spider that eats plants. It lives on acacia trees and survives on tasty leaf tips and nectar from the tree's flowers.

## TWIST IT!

Lunch!

A spider assassin's long neck helps it to get its jaws closer to its prey.

Chelicerae

## Spider assassin

This spider belongs to a strange group of arachnids from the island of Madagascar. It's a member of the Archaeidae family, which all have extremely long chelicerae (jaws). The spider, known as a spider assassin, uses its chelicerae like spears and plunges them into its prey.

These spiders only hunt other spiders.

A spider's venom paralyzes its prey —stopping it from moving.

## Fangs!

At the end of some spiders' chelicerae are long fangs, which are connected to a venom gland. When the spider bites, venom flows through the hollow fang and into the victim's body.

## Hands, jaws, or claws?

All spiders have a pair of **chelicerae**—body parts that are positioned around their mouth. Chelicerae are sometimes described as a spider's hands because they can hold or move things. They are as powerful as jaws and are often lined with little "teeth" so they can crush as well as bite. Some spiders use their chelicerae to mash their prey into a mush before they eat it.

Chelicerae

**BIG WORD ALERT**

**VENOM**

An animal poison that is injected by stinging or biting.

Fangs

Pedipalps

## How spiders eat

★ A spider grabs its prey with its arm-like pedipalps and moves it toward its jaw-like chelicerae.

★ The spider plunges its fangs into the prey, and injects venom that paralyzes the prey and stops it from moving.

★ Once the prey is still, the spider vomits acid-like juices all over it.

★ The juices dissolve the prey's insides, which the spider sucks out through the bite holes made by the fangs.

Acidic vomit!

# IT'S UN-BEE-LIEVABLE

## Workers unite!

Bees, wasps, and hornets all belong to the same family of insects and most of them have a nasty stinger in the tail.

Honeybees live in colonies of up to 100,000 bees. Most honeybees are worker females that look after the queen and her young, tidy the hive, defend the nest, and collect nectar and pollen from flowers to feed the colony. Male bees are called drones, and their job is to mate with the queen to produce new bees for the hive.

## Sweet treat

Bees make honey so they can store food over the winter. It is made from flower nectar (a sweet liquid made by flowers to attract insects), which mixes with chemicals inside the bee's stomach. The bees spit the nectar into wax cells inside the hive, and fan it with their wings to turn the paste into honey. Honey can last for many years!

## TWIST IT!

## BEE-LIEVE IT!

Some bees live in enormous colonies, making their homes in large hives. Paper wasps also live in groups, and make their nests out of chewed up wood and spit. Other bee and wasp species live alone.

A bee can visit up to 100 flowers during every trip out of the hive.

Paper wasps can recognize each other by their faces. Scientists think they might be as good at recognizing faces as humans.

## Super sting!

Only females have stings because each stinger is made from the part of the female's body that is used for laying eggs. Wasp stings are smooth, so they can be plunged into a victim and pulled out again without damaging the wasp itself. Honeybee stings are barbed (they have little hooks) so when the bee tries to pull the stinger out, it rips from its body. The bee dies soon afterward.

# Ripley explains... Wasp, bee, or hornet?

They look similar, but they do have their differences.

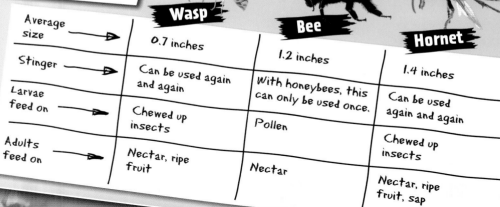

| | Wasp | Bee | Hornet |
|---|---|---|---|
| Average size | 0.7 inches | 1.2 inches | 1.4 inches |
| Stinger | Can be used again and again | With honeybees, this can only be used once. | Can be used again and again |
| Larvae feed on | Chewed up insects | Pollen | Chewed up insects |
| Adults feed on | Nectar, ripe fruit | Nectar | Nectar, ripe fruit, sap |

## Master mimic

Yellow and black stripes warn other animals that bees and wasps can sting. Some flies have copied the striped pattern as protection. When one animal pretends to be another it is called a mimic.

This neon cuckoo bee has a blue and black furry body.

## BLUE BEE!

Not all bees are black and yellow. Some species, such as this cuckoo bee, are different colors. Cuckoo bees may look pretty, but they lead a nasty life. Instead of collecting their own pollen and making their own nests, they let others do all the work. A cuckoo bee lays its egg in another bee's nest and when the larva hatches, it eats the pollen that was intended for the host bee's larva, which starves to death soon after hatching.

A hexagon-shaped hole in a hive is a brood cell, where an egg is laid and a larva develops, or it is used for making and storing honey.

## Ripley's Believe It or Not!

Bees at a cluster of beehives in France produced honey in unusual shades of blue and green! Their keepers believe residue from containers of M&M's® candy at a nearby factory was the cause.

# BEAUTIES AND THE BEASTS

## Look at me!

Feast your eyes on our catwalk of the world's most glamorous spiders in their gorgeous colors, but you might want to look away from some of their less attractive cousins!

Some of these spiders are eight-legged beauties, while others give us the creeps!

## BEAUTIES

Most spiders like to hide, but these super stunner spiders have a good reason to show off. They are males that use their good looks to attract females, which are drab and dull by comparison.

### Peacock spider

When handsome peacock spider males want a mate, they don't rely on just their looks to win a female's heart. They also like to wave their legs at her, and perform a little love dance!

### Mirror spider

Mirror spiders look as if they are coated in shiny sequins. The dazzling patches on their body may be used to reflect light to confuse predators.

# BEASTS

Beauty is in the eye of the beholder, but not even a mother could find these freaky faces attractive! Having an ugly mug doesn't bother these spiders, though. Who needs to look good when you have big fangs and deadly venom?

## House spider

House spiders may be ugly up-close but they are harmless—except to the annoying flies that like to buzz around our food and spread diseases, which they kill and eat! House spiders are the good guys in the spider world, keeping our homes pest-free.

## Curved spiny orb weaver

Some spiders are show-offs and not shy. This spider is so bright and bold that predators are sure to spot it. Those colors and extremely long spines probably scare predators away.

### Ripley's Believe It or Not!®

This spider is known as the happy face spider! Found in the rainforests of the Hawaiian Islands, the tiny spider is thought to be harmless to humans.

# MORTAL COMBAT

## Creepy-crawly killers

Most spiders and creepy crawlies may look scary, but they are, in fact, our friends not our enemies. However, there are some brutal beasties around, with lethal stings and bites, and dirty habits.

Watching bugs and spiders in action is fascinating. It is a great way to learn more about our natural world. Most are harmless, but avoid touching them unless you know what they are. There is no reason to kill most spiders and creepy crawlies—leave them alone and they will leave you alone! Here's our collection of some of nature's nasties.

## Ant-snatching assassin bug

This is a particularly creepy insect that likes to keep safe by making itself a gruesome "corpse cloak" out of dead ants! Scientists think that it covers itself with the stacked up bodies of dead ants to disguise it from predators such as spiders.

### Kiss of death

All assassin bugs, which are also known as kissing bugs, have sharp mouthparts that they use to pierce the skin of their victims. They carry the potentially deadly Chagas disease, which infects about 8 million people in the world.

A mosquito can pierce its victim's skin and feed on their blood without being noticed.

## Mosquitoes

The females of some types of mosquito feed on human blood when it is time for them to lay their eggs. As they feed, they can spread terrible diseases including malaria. Malaria kills about 660,000 people every year, most of them children.

Bluebottles and greenbottles are types of blowfly.

TWIST IT!

The venom of a black widow spider is 15 times more toxic than a rattlesnake's venom.

Not many scorpions can deliver a sting that kills people, but a deathstalker scorpion's venom is powerful enough to kill a child.

The venom of a brown recluse spider is unlikely to kill a human, but it can destroy the flesh around the bite.

When a kissing bug bites, it injects a liquid into the victim's flesh, turning it into a soupy mixture that the bug can suck up.

## SMALL BUT DEADLY

## Blowflies

These flies have foul habits. They feed on dead animals and poop, and like to lay their eggs on our food. Blowflies can spread diseases that cause stomach upsets or more serious illness. Some even burrow into the flesh of animals and humans to lay their eggs.

Black widows can be recognized by the "hourglass" red markings on their abdomen.

## Black widows

Black widows and funnel web spiders are two of the world's deadliest spiders. Funnel webs are very aggressive, especially when the males are hunting for a mate. Black widows are shy, so they are less dangerous.

These blood flukes have been removed from a person's intestine.

### BIG WORD ALERT
### PARASITE
An animal that lives on, or in, another animal and does it harm.

## Fluke worms

Flukes are worm-like animals and parasites. They live in water, but burrow their way into the bodies of other animals to lay their eggs. Blood flukes infect about 200 million people around the world, causing diseases such as bilharzia, which make people very ill.

# BUGS IN DANGER

## BREAKING NEWS

**Our planet needs its spiders and other creepy crawlies, but did you know that some of them are in danger of dying out? What is threatening the world of little animals, and what can you do to help them?**

### What's so great about all these bugs?

- Spiders eat flies that spread diseases.
- Bugs are food for bigger animals, such as birds.
- They clear up dead animals and plants.
- They pollinate plants.
- They can be a good source of food for humans.

### What if we didn't have them?

- We'd run short of food pretty quickly, and so would lots of other animals.
- There would be no chocolate, fruit, or honey!
- We'd be knee-deep in dead bodies and poop before long.
- The world would be bugless but BORING!

## How you can help

If you have a garden, grow plants that encourage lots of different types of wildlife.

### Who'll spot the last one?

This fluffy fellow is on his last legs, and having eight of them won't make his future any brighter. Ladybug spiders are so rare that scientists predict their days are numbered. The problem is that these gorgeous creatures live on heathland in northern Europe—a special habitat that humans have been destroying.

Can this precious spider keep its foothold on the future, or is it destined to go the way of the dodo and become extinct?

### Why are bugs in danger?

There are some simple reasons that bugs and spiders are in danger, and we could deal with them all, if we wanted to:

- When farmers cover a large area with one type of crop, such as palm oil, the number of species of invertebrates falls. This means there is less BIODIVERSITY, which is a BAD THING.
- Pesticides may be useful for getting rid of pests but they often kill good bugs too. Pesticides can get into rivers, killing animals there as well.
- Habitat loss is a big problem for all animals. If we take away their homes, to farm or build on, they don't usually find another place to live—they die instead.

# WHAT'S THE BUZZ ABOUT BEES?

Bees and flies pollinate flowers, which means they take pollen from one plant to another, so fruit and seeds can grow. The number of bees has fallen, and scientists and farmers are worried. No one knows why the bees are dying, but it is possible it is because of pesticides—chemicals used on crops to control insect pests.

## HUMAN BEE-INGS!

In China, farmers have killed so many insects with their pesticides that there are large areas where there are none left to pollinate the fruit trees. Humans now have to do the job by hand!

## BIG WORD ALERT
### BIODIVERSITY
The variety of living things found in a particular place.

## Time to say goodbye?

The dazzling peacock parachute spider can't rely on its good looks any more. This may be one of the most beautiful animals to walk the Earth, but it faces a bleak future. That's thanks to the destruction of its forest home, and "pet traders" who capture spiders to sell as pets.

Found in just one Indian forest, the rare peacock parachute spider needs our help to survive.

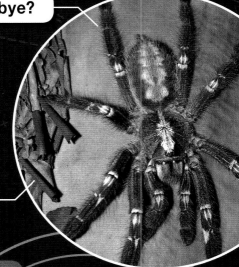

# What can we do to save our bugs?

Take part in local wildlife watches, where you can learn more about the little animals, how to identify them, and keep records of when you see them.

Don't disturb their habitat. Respect them and teach other people why they matter.

Support businesses and places that protect the environment.

Visit nature reserves where the land is being saved for all animals—big and small.

# INDEX

**Bold** numbers refer to main entries; numbers in *italic* refer to illustrations

# ACKNOWLEDGMENTS

**COVER** (sp) Rex/Tomas Rax/Solent News, (t) Caters News Agency Ltd.; **2** (t/l) © spotwin - istock.com; **3** (t/l) Rex/F1 Online, (b/r) Rex/Lessy Sebastian/Solent News; **4** Rex/Tomas Rax/Solent News; **5** (t) Rex/Mohamed Babu/Solent News; **6** (b/l) © Dave Allen Photography - istock.com, (b/c) © tacojim - istock.com, (b/r) © johnandersonphoto - istock.com; **6–7** (dp) Nicky Bay, sgmacro.blogspot.com; **7** (c/r) © Serhiy Kobyakov - shutterstock.com, (b/l) April Noble/www.AntWeb.org, (b/c/l) © Barry Mansell/naturepl.com, (b/c/r) © Henrik_L - istock.com, (b/r) © cosmln - istock.com; **8** (l) © Raffalo - istock.com, (r) © alslutsky - shutterstock.com, (b) © Henrik_L - istock.com; **9** (t) © Hugh Lansdown - shutterstock.com, (c/r) Gustoimages/Science Photo Library, (b) Dave Roberts/Science Photo Library; **10–11** (dp) Nicky Bay, sgmacro.blogspot.com; **11** (t) AFP/Getty Images, (b) Rex/Lessy Sebastian/Solent News; **12** (b) © Kim Taylor/naturepl.com; **12–13** (dp) Brian Valentine; **13** (c/r) Mitshuiko Imamori/Minden Pictures/National Geographic Creative, (b) Nicky Bay, sgmacro.blogspot.com; **14** (b) © Visuals Unlimited/naturepl.com; **14–15** (dp) © Ingo Arndt/naturepl.com; **15** (r, t) © NHPA/Photoshot; **16** (b) © Bence Mate/naturepl.com; **16–17** (dp) Yanuar Akbar/Caters News; **17** (t) Jessica Dickson, (b/l) © Pan Xunbin - shutterstock.com, (b/c) © Henrik_L - istock.com, (b/r) © Antagain - istock.com; **18** (t/r) Nicky Bay, sgmacro.blogspot.com, (b/l) Rocket Design, (b/r) © Stephen Dalton/naturepl.com; **19** (t/l) Nicky Bay, sgmacro.blogspot.com, (t/r) © Nick Garbutt/naturepl.com, (b) © UPPA/Photoshot; **20** (c) Rex/Hans Christoph Kappel/Nature Picture Library, (b) © Stephen Dalton naturepl.com; **21** (t/l) © NHPA/Photoshot, (r) © nyiragongo - fotolia.com, (c) © Kim Taylor/naturepl.com, (b) © Nature Production/naturepl.com; **22–23** Nicky Bay, sgmacro.blogspot.com; **24** (b/l, b/r) © Rolf Nussbaumer/naturepl.com; **24–25** (dp) © stanley45 - istock.com; **25** (b/l, b/c, b/r) © vblinov - istock.com; **26** © Nick Garbutt/naturepl.com; **27** (t/l) © a-wrangler - istock.com, (t/r) © FourOaks - istock.com, (b) Natural History Museum, London/Science Photo Library; **28** (t) © Alex Hyde/naturepl.com, (b) Nicky Bay, sgmacro.blogspot.com; **29** (t) Nicky Bay, sgmacro.blogspot.com, (b) John Mitchell/Science Photo Library; **30** (t/r) Imagebroker/FLPA; **31** (t) © Dietmar Nill/naturepl.com, (c) © Jane Burton/naturepl.com, (b) © temmuz can arsiray - istock.com; **32** (t) Nicky Bay, sgmacro.blogspot.com, (b) © NHPA/Photoshot; **33** (t) Micky Lim, Singapore (http://www.flickr.com/photos/mickylim/), (c) Martin Dohrn Science Photo Library, (b/l) © CathyKeifer - istock.com, (b/r) Nicky Bay, sgmacro.blogspot.com; **34** (sp) © Jouan & Rius/naturepl.com, (b/l) Nicky Bay, sgmacro.blogspot.com; **35** (t) © Premaphotos/naturepl.com, (b) Emanuele Biggi/FLPA; **36** Paul Bertner; **37** (t) © Dietmar Nill/naturepl.com, (b) Nicky Bay, sgmacro.blogspot.com; **38** (b) © Alex Hyde/naturepl.com; **38–39** (dp) © tr3gin - shutterstock.com; **39** (t/l, t/r) © irin-k - shutterstock.com, (t/c) © paulrommer - shutterstock.com, (c) Nicky Bay, sgmacro.blogspot.com, (b) Reuters/Vincent Kessler; **40** (l) Nicky Bay, sgmacro.blogspot.com, (t/r) Jürgen Otto; **41** (t) Rex/F1 Online, (b/l) Nicky Bay, sgmacro.blogspot.com, (b/r) Caters News Agency Ltd.; **42** (c) Nicky Bay, sgmacro.blogspot.com, (b) © smuay - shutterstock.com; **43** (t) © Meul/Arco/naturepl.com, (l) © spotwin - istock.com, (r) Sinclair Stammers/Science Photo Library; **44** (t) © Hyena Reality - shutterstock.com, (b) © Ingo Arndt/naturepl.com; **45** (t/r) © Srabin - istock.com, (l) © ilfede - istock.com, (r) Rick. C West

**Key: t = top, b = bottom, c = center, l = left, r = right, sp = single page, dp = double page, bgd = background**

All other photos are from Ripley's Entertainment Inc. All other artwork by Rocket Design (East Anglia) Ltd.

Every attempt has been made to acknowledge correctly and contact copyright holders and we apologize in advance for any unintentional errors or omissions, which will be corrected in future editions.

TWISTS